Bruce King

COLD CALLING

-

EVERYTHING YOU NEED TO KNOW TO BECOME WORLD CLASS AT TELE – SALES AND APPOINTMENT SETTING

MADE EASY

www.bruceking.co.uk

Cold Calling

Bruce King

Crown House Publishing
23 Southerton Way, Shenley,
Hertfordshire WD7 9LJ
United Kingdom

ISBN 978-1518891007

Cold Calling

Contents

About the author - Bruce King

Bruce King has more than thirty years experience working with organisations from SMEs to major international companies and speaking to audiences around the world on the subjects of sales, marketing and achieving greater results in any area of their business and personal lives.

Bruce King's earliest career was in the field of complimentary medicine and personal growth. He qualified as a nutritional consultant and acupuncturist and studied and taught numerous powerful, personal growth and personal development techniques. He established one of the UK's first multi-disciplinary complimentary medical centres, had his own radio programme on Radio London and wrote articles on alternative medicine and personal growth for numerous national magazines. He was also one of the first people in the UK to run seminars teaching people how to walk across a bed of burning coals.

After several successful years in the complimentary medical field, Bruce decided he needed a new challenge. He sold the medical centre and, by what he describes as "a bizarre series of coincidences", he embarked upon a career in sales. He studied with some of the world's top sales coaches and had an extremely successful and profitable career selling and managing sales teams for some of the UK's top companies. Bruce puts a great deal of his success, and the success of those who worked with him, down to the strategies he learned and taught in his background in the personal development field.

Over the years Bruce has developed several successful and, in some cases, award winning businesses which he has subsequently sold. He has worked with sales teams to achieve a frequently extraordinary increase in sales and coached business owners to help them to create more successful and profitable enterprises.

In 1994 Bruce wrote his first book. Titled 'Psycho-Selling – Double Your Income From Sales In 8 Weeks', the book was published by the prestigious publisher BBC Books and became an international best seller. It launched Bruce's career as an international conference speaker.

Since then he has written several other best selling books including Double Your Sales, published by FT Prentice Hall, Winning Sales Referrals, published by Soderpalm Publishing, Smash Your Goals published by Crown House Publishing and others. He has produced several training videos and CDs and has been presenting keynote speeches and Sales Master Classes around the world.

There is more information on all Bruce King's books and other training materials at www.bruceking.co.uk.

Of equal importance, although only a spare time activity, in 2012 Bruce started writing books to inspire children to grow up to be the very best they can be and to help raise money for children's charities. The first titled 'How To Be A Super Bear' became a No. 1 Best Seller and there have been several more published since then.

Introduction

Those of you who have read my recent book titled 'How To Double Your Sales will know that in many industries and professions I have always found that referral marketing and networking are far more effective ways of generating new clients and new business than cold calling. Having said that, I also recognize that in some industries you can only sell on the telephone and in some industries and professions, cold calling, either to make a sale or an appointment to sell, is an absolute necessity. The purpose of this book is to teach you the techniques I have learned and taught to thousands of others that can enable you to become World-Class at telephone sales and appointment setting.

I well remember my very first job as a full-time salesperson. It was over thirty years ago and I had just joined the financial services industry. I had completed my technical induction training at the head office training centre and was back in the office for the first time since my original interview. I was now a fully qualified Financial Advisor and my job was to sell Life Insurance, Pension Plans and Savings Plans. I use the word 'job' although there was no salary, no car and indeed no benefits of any kind. It was sell or starve!

Now picture the scene: A predominantly large open plan office meant to cope with forty-five financial advisors. There were eight small cubicles down one side of the room for the star performers – the high flyers of financial services – the big earners! The rest of the room was a clutter of odd tables, some with chairs and some without. Some had telephones and some did not. The first few people to arrive at the office got a table, chair and telephone. Some got a table and telephone and some got nothing! Overlooking the entire shabby arrangement was the manager's office, built on a dais, so he could view everything that was going on through his office window. I remember saying to myself on my first day – "what am I doing here?"

I was first in that morning and asked the manager what I should be doing to get started. I asked if there was going to be any marketing or sales training. His reply was to give me a copy of Yellow Pages and the instruction to just start calling people and asking for an appointment. That was it! No suggestions as to whom to call, what to say or any other advice and no offer of any training. It was going to be sink or swim!

It took me four weeks of calling strangers for six hours a day, six days a week before I made my first appointment, and when I went on that appointment they were not available.

I resolved to become one of those star performers. I wanted one of those small, private cubicles, away from the clutter of that horrible open plan office and the non-positive conversations going on all around me. I also knew that I was going to have to learn to do it myself - and I did. I read dozens of books on sales and marketing, invested my own time and money on sales training courses and applied the personal growth techniques I had developed over the preceding years and which you can read about in my other books. Within seven months I was sitting in my private cubicle and I was amongst the top three 'star performers' in that office.

That was many years ago, and since then I have coached thousands of people to sell over the telephone and to set sales appointments over the telephone across a diverse range of industries and professions. I've coached salespeople who sell over the telephone to sell advertising, office supplies, cars, delivery services, electrical supplies, financial services, gardening equipment, hairdressing supplies, insurance, kitchen supplies, life insurance, pet supplies and stocks and shares – to name but a few. I've even coached salespeople to sell apartments costing over £300,000 as tax shelters without the customer even visiting the property.

When it comes to appointment setting, I've coached people from just about every industry or profession you can think of to set appointments, either for themselves or for other people. Some of the people I have coached have even given up their position they were working in at the time to become professional appointment setters for others and earned more doing this than they were earning in their previous position. So whatever it is that you are selling, you too can achieve a rapid improvement in your results by following the techniques I set out in this program.

Cold Calling

1. What is Cold Calling?

Cold calling can be simply defined as 'a telephone call being made to someone who was not expecting your call'.

It does not matter if you had written to them beforehand and are following up that e-mail and/or the brochure you sent them. If it was an e-mail, it may not have been opened or even reached them. If it was a letter, it may have been lost in the post or not passed on to them by somebody opening their mail. Even if they had seen it, the content may not have been of interest. Even if it was of interest, they may not recall receiving it when you make the call and they may not remember your name. It's still a cold call and the rules of engagement apply.

It does not matter if the person you are calling is a referral from another person. There's no guarantee at all that they will remember your name or your company's name when you make the call, even if the person who referred you had told them to expect a call from you. It's still a cold call and the rules of engagement apply.

It does not even matter if they were eagerly expecting your call. If their PA, or other gatekeeper, has not been informed by them to put you through, it's still a cold call and the rules of engagement apply.

Just to be really clear, if the person you are calling does not know you or recall your name after a quick reminder from you as to why they should – it's a cold call and the rules of engagement apply. But before we engage with the person we are cold calling, there's a lot of preparatory work to do; so let's get started.

2. Getting in the right frame of mind

You've almost certainly heard the expression – 'it's all in the mind'. Well it is! So let's get started by dealing with your mind first of all - what's going on in it and how to change it for the better.

People I have met who have to sell on the telephone or make appointments over the telephone fall into a number of categories, and often several:

- They hate it
- They are scared of doing it
- They don't mind doing it because they know or hope it's going to get them to where they want to be
- They really like it or even love it.

Which category or categories do you fall into?

If you hate it…

If you hate it, cannot get to like it or do not even want to, then best you quit and find another way of selling, prospecting or get another job or career. Life is too short to be doing something you hate and you will never do it well.

If you're scared of doing it…

If you're scared of doing it, then I know why. It's because you fear rejection! So let's look at this issue of fear first of all.

Cold Calling

Some years ago, when I was working full time in sales, I was driving past a large office block which had the name 'Rogers & Associates – Accountants' on the face of the building in large letters. At the time, I was selling accounting systems for accountants and my first reaction was to stop and call in to introduce myself. Then fear set in.

The little voice in my head was recalling past times when I had dropped in without an appointment and had been rejected, or had the opportunity to show them what I was selling and was told it was of no interest. I imagined how it would all be a waste of time.

As a result of those thoughts, I kept driving. However, after a few hundred yards I put the brake on my thoughts, turned the car around, drove back and dropped in. It transpired that the senior partner was an old college friend of mine. We had coffee, caught up on old times and, to cut a long story short, a few weeks later I received an order that earned me over four thousand pounds in commission.

The truth of the matter is that most of the things we fear are just in our imagination. According to some psychologists 'fear' stands for **F**antasized **E**xperiences **A**ppearing **R**eal. In other words, the experiences we imagine may happen or they may not happen, but by imaging that they will, we create fear.

If you don't believe me, take out half an hour and list as many situations as you can think of when you were scared of what might happen if you did something - but you did it just the same. Then place a tick against those situations where what you feared would happen, did happen. I'm betting there are going to be very few ticks! Of course when it comes to cold calling, you are almost certainly going to get a lot more rejection than in other areas of sales, but if you know your 'numbers', which I'll deal with later, then this won't bother you anymore.

Our Stone Age ancestors used fear as a way of dealing with dangerous situations. It was part of the 'fight or flight' mechanism that helped to keep them safe and the fear created an adrenaline rush that enabled them to deal with the danger. Nowadays, we do not have to deal with the dangers that our ancestors experienced. Today fear is a signal to us that we must be cautious, alert and ready to deal with a specific situation, and we experience the same or a similar adrenaline rush. However, because we do not have to fight or fly, we transfer our fear into situations where we really need not be fearful at all. In spite of that, it is almost guaranteed you are going to experience fear frequently in your life. It is how you face up to it and how you deal with it that will make the difference between failure and success.

How we deal with fear is a choice!

How we deal with fear is a choice we always make for ourselves. Sometimes we choose to face fear head on and we are exhilarated by it and love the experience. Other times we allow it to freeze us into inactivity. For example: Did you ever go on one of those real scary roller coaster rides? You were possibly petrified when you were queuing for the ride – but you went anyway! You chose to be excited!

Do you snow ski? Do you ever get scared when approaching a new and slightly more dangerous run than you are used to? I know you do and I know that most times, if not always, you choose to ski it anyway. You choose to be excited!

How you deal with fear is a choice; so why not always choose to be excited and exhilarated by it? Fear is not something to be feared; it can be your greatest ally. Fear is a natural reaction and not something you should feel at all ashamed of admitting. Accept that being fearful is a natural stage in the process of achieving great success. Face the fear with courage and know that eventually, if you do this, you cannot fail to achieve your goals.

Dealing with rejection

Now some sales coaches will tell you that rejection has nothing to do with you and that the customer or potential customer is just rejecting your product or service. That's rubbish! I can think of many reasons why someone would reject YOU when you call them. These could include:

- You pronounced their name incorrectly
- It was obvious they were very busy and you should have acknowledged that and said you would call back at another time

- You were rude to them
- You were rude to their PA or secretary
- You interrupted them
- You didn't listen
- You ignored their 'objections'
- You were unprofessional
- You spoke badly
- You spoke like it was just another cold call you were making
- You sounded disinterested in what they had to say and just wanted to get on with what you had to say
- You didn't seem to understand their issues or know your product or service and what it could do for them

And the list goes on!

So what I'd like you to do is make a list of all the reasons why people may have rejected YOU in the past and, by the time you have finished this program, determine how you will conduct yourself in the future to avoid this ever happening again.

Make this list now on the following page or a separate sheet (or sheets).

Reasons Prospects Have Rejected ME In The Past – Be Honest!

So let's now discuss how to deal with rejection if it wasn't YOU who was being rejected but rather your product or service. Instead of thinking about the outcome of your call as being to make a sale or make an appointment, you need to put this into a totally different perspective.

When you make a telephone call, no matter how carefully you have done your research into the prospect, if indeed you have had the time or opportunity to do any at all, nine hundred and ninety-nine times out of one thousand, you have absolutely no idea whether or not your prospect has any real need for your product or service at that time. So instead of thinking the outcome for your call should be to make a sale or an appointment, you should look at the purpose of your call as to establish whether or not your prospect has a need for your product or service. Then, providing you have presented to them professionally and purposefully, you always come out with a positive outcome and you can move on to making the next call in a positive frame of mind.

And finally, remember this: **Rejection never leaves you any worse off than before you were rejected.**

How you perceive yourself is how others will perceive you too...

How you think, and behave as a result, is a critical factor in how others perceive you when you telephone them.

Cold Calling

One of the conscious and subconscious challenges we face when we cold call is based on the fact that we have all been on the receiving end of many terrible cold calls ourselves. When I'm in the office and not too busy, I ask for all cold telephone calls to be put through to me. I like listening to what are in most cases appalling, but occasionally brilliant pitches. Here are two examples of appalling ones and you will note that when the approach is bad, I can be rather difficult:

Caller: Is that Mr King?

Me: Yes.

Caller: How are you today? (I simply hate that question from a total stranger on a cold call – it's so very insincere. The only stranger who is entitled to ask that of me is a doctor).

Me: Absolutely awful thank you.

Caller: Excellent! I'm calling from the XYZ Company - would you be interested in buying CCTV?

Me: No.

Caller: Thank you (hung up).

And…

Caller: I'm calling to speak to the owner of the business.

Me: We have 27,000 shareholders all of whom own the business. Which one would you like to speak with? (not true – me just being difficult again).

Caller: Oh – anyone who is available please.

Me: None of them work here. They are just owners and shareholders. Do you have the name of the person you need to speak with?

Caller: I just wanted to speak with the owner.

Me: What's it about?

Caller: It's private.

Me: Which company do you represent – who are you calling on behalf of please?

Caller: It's private. I can't tell you.

Me: Well I might be able to put you through to someone who could help if you can tell me what it's about.

Caller: I can't – it's private for the owner.

Me: Tell you what. I'll promise not to tell your boss you told me what it's about. Then when you do, I may be able to put you through to the right person.

Caller: (Silence for a while followed by hang up).

The truth of the matter is that good cold callers are so rare that we think we are all tarred with the same brush. We think we know how people are going to react to a cold call before we have even dialed the number and we expect a similar outcome to those who make such bad calls. **And what you expect is what you get – most of the time!**

Now think back to a time when you received a really excellent cold call and your positive response, or you listened to a real professional make one and get a positive response. It was a whole different ball game wasn't it!

Cold Calling is NOT a 'numbers game'

Let's dispel one final myth relating to attitude before we move on. I've heard so many people refer to cold calling as 'just a numbers game'. They treat it in the same way as untargeted Junk Mail. Make the calls, in the same old, same old way and eventually, someone will say 'yes'. That's the wrong attitude!

Of course if you keep records, as I'll explain how to do later in this program, then you count the numbers, BUT the numbers can be massively improved upon as you improve your skills. I've coached telephone sales and marketing people the same skills I'm teaching you on this program, and in many cases, results have improved by five hundred per cent and more!

So from now on, and with the help of this program, set yourself up to think and act like a true professional cold caller and expect to get great results.

The Key Attributes of World-Class Achievers

I have worked with World-Class Achievers for many years and here are the three simple to follow and key attributes that have contributed most of all to their success. They are equally appropriate to becoming World-Class when it comes to telephone sales and appointment setting.

Persistence - Persistence is incompatible with failure

Commitment - Commitment is incompatible with failure.

Determination - Determination is incompatible with failure.

If you would like to learn more of the techniques I teach people to achieve great success in any aspect of their business and personal lives, invest in my book titled 'Smash Your Goals'.

Cold Calling

3. Equipment & Environment

Your Office Space

I appreciate that you don't always have complete control over your working environment and, believe me, I've seen telephone salespeople working in some dreadful places in the past. Fortunately this happens far less often nowadays. But if you have a choice, do make sure it is as conducive to high and successful productivity as possible. **Some key points:**

- Fresh air
- Not too hot – not too cold
- Some uplifting pictures and slogans on the walls
- Your own 'goal board'
- As quiet as possible so you are not distracted (and the prospect is not distracted by background noise)
- An uncluttered desk; just have all you need close by for the task in hand

And the three most important items of all:

1: A Headset. It's an absolute essential for cold calling for several reasons. You must have your hands free to be able to carry out other tasks whilst you are making your calls without holding the telephone with your shoulder and cheek. Not only will this give you a stiff neck but, more importantly, it affects your posture, your voice and the way you communicate and come across to your prospect.

When you are speaking on the telephone, my Number One rule is that you should always act as if you were actually sitting down with that prospect. You never do anything you would not do if you were not there and you do everything you would do if you were there. You wear the same expression on your face as if you were there and you gesticulate and use mannerisms as if you were there. You cannot do that with a telephone in one hand and a mouse or pen in the other (or indeed juggling the two) if you are not wearing a headset. I have consulted to organizations who have achieved a twenty per cent plus increase in sales just by replacing handsets with headsets on my advice.

2: A Mirror so that you can check the expression on your face and, ideally, with a notice above it with the word SMILE written in bold print.

3: A Monitoring System – actually two!

The first of your two systems is a CRM or Customer Relationship Management System. This is used to keep track of your prospects, their contact details, details of their business, the key people around them such as their secretary or PA, your progress to date with them, date and time of next call and any other important points you should make note of, all accessible in one place.

There are very effective CRM computer based systems you can use or it could be as simple as a card box system. Of course the computer based systems are going to be far more sophisticated than a box stuffed with index cards, but I know some really top salespeople who still use a card box system and are amongst the top performers in their field. As Zig Ziglar once said, *"I don't care what system you use, so long as you have a system!"*

The second system is a Results Monitor – RM for short. These are built into some of the most sophisticated CRM systems but, in most cases, are not as comprehensive and effective as a paper based system or a spreadsheet. It won't take you long to set one up and the benefits are extraordinary.

The purpose of an RM is to track your results at each stage of the telephone call; to show you areas where you may need to coach yourself or get coached on the particular skill needed for that part of the process; to monitor how you are improving and most importantly – to know the results you are getting. In a moment I'll go through the structure of the paper based system or spreadsheet, but first of all, and to demonstrate why it's so important, let's go right to the end.

Let's suppose that you have been tracking the results of your cold calling for twenty hours. From the RM system, you have worked out the following statistics:

It took 2 dials to get an answer from anyone to the call you make (a contact)

It took 4 dials to get through to a Decision Maker's PA or Secretary

It took 3 conversations with a PA or Secretary to get put through to a Decision Maker

It took 5 conversations with a Decision Maker to get an appointment to see one of them

Your stats from your meeting records show the average meeting (whether you sell at all of them or not) generates a sale to the value of £2400.

So working that backwards, it takes 60 cold telephone calls to earn £2,400, which equates to £40 per cold call.

Of course your statistics will be different for a number of reasons and your sales process may be rather different. You'll be working out your own statistics in the future, but let's suppose those were your statistics. Does it shed a rather different light on the picture when you work out that you have earned £40 per cold call? And to put it in a different perspective…

Suppose I were to pay you £40 every time you picked up the telephone and dialed a number. What time would you get into the office in the morning and start cold calling? How often would you take a break? How often would you wander off for a conversation with a colleague? How late would you stay into the evening? And……has the penny dropped?

On a following page is an example of a RM spreadsheet. It might work for you as it is, or you may need to re-design it for your particular purpose. For example you might want to add a column for Messages Left on Voice Mail and another for Voicemail Messages Returned. It's up to you to adjust this sample to make it work for you.

The column headings on my example mean the following and you should place a tick in each box if you achieved the task:

DIAL – dialed a number

CONTACT – someone answered the telephone

DM – they put you through to the Decision Maker

INTRO – you introduced yourself in brief to the DM and got permission to continue

PITCH – you got through your presentation without the call being terminated

APPT – appointment made (not necessary if you are selling on the telephone)

SALE - that's obvious as is SALE VALUE.

Cold Calling

DIAL	CONTACT	DM	INTRO	PITCH	APPT	SALE	£

Time Started: Time finished:

At the end of each session or day, you total the number of ticks in each column and interpret the results. So let's take a look at two completed RMs: one for Appointment Setting and the other for Telephone Sales, and just use the Headers and Totals to work from.

Appointment Setting RM

DIAL	CONTACT	DM	INTRO	PITCH	APPT MADE
60	45	12	6	3	1

We could deduce the following from this:

- If business-to-business, this is not a good list if 15 were gone away.
- You need to improve your skills with PAs and Secretaries to get them to put you through. Of course the DM could be out or in a meeting and you might wish to add a column to the RM sheet headed NA (Not Available) and another for PCB (Permission to Call Back).
- You should examine your opening statement. Fifty per cent were not allowing you to continue.
- Ask yourself is one appointment in three pitches acceptable? Could it be improved upon?

Telephone Selling RM

DIAL	CONTACT	DM	INTRO	PITCH	SALE	SALE VALUE £
60	59	12	11	3	0	0

What will you deduce from these results? (Answers not supplied)

4. Time Management Techniques For Cold Calling

If you are not cold calling all day, and just need to, or have to, make calls as part of your overall responsibilities, then you must set aside specific times for doing this and build that time into your overall plan for your working week. It must NOT be done when you have a few spare minutes or you 'just feel like it now' or you suddenly find yourself short of appointments.

So when is the best time to allocate to your cold calling sessions? A lot depends upon your individual body rhythm. There are times of the day when you feel at your best, most productive and most energetic. For some people that's first thing in the morning, for others it's mid morning or mid afternoon and for the very few, it's late in the day. What is the time of the day that you feel at your best, most productive and most energetic?

When you have decided what time of the day you should allocate to your calls, set aside that time in your planner. I recommend an absolute minimum of one hour without a break. Your call list, monitoring systems and any other literature or sales aids you might need to refer to should be close at hand – as of course should be your script. (If the thought of a script strikes you with horror, I hope you will change your mind when I deal with scripts later in the program). The aim should be to have everything available to you so that you can continuously dial and speak, without interruption, for at least one hour. That means no tea or coffee for that hour, no snacking, in fact not even putting down the telephone. It should be one call after the other. You can tidy up your notes, send e-mails and letters and reward yourself for a job well done later.

I also recommend you plan to have regular cold calling sessions. The more often you have them and the more practice you get, the more you monitor your results, the better you are going to be and the better the results you are going to get.

The best times to call Decision Makers

Aside from the fact that there is a time in the day when you feel at your best, there are also times in the day when it is easier to get through to people on your contact list, particularly Decision Makers higher up in the target organization. If your target is people at that level, be aware that they often tend to get in earlier than their 'gatekeepers' and stay later and may well answer the telephone themselves. So set aside some time in those hours to make those calls.

Two other Time Management techniques

I am also going to share with you the two simple time management techniques, which I use to manage my time and which are the most effective that I know. These techniques are equally appropriate for people in any career as they are for people in sales.

Technique 1 – TWF (The Waste Factor)

One of the questions I often ask my audiences is: "As a percentage of your working day, how much time do you honestly admit to wasting or allowing other people to waste for you?" I ask them to write the answer down on a small piece of paper, fold it up so that their colleagues cannot see it, and then pass it down the row to the end where I have helpers collect them all. They are then put in a large box and I take twenty out of the box at random and read out the figures. I'd like you to write your figure down now before reading on.

The average time that those twenty people whose pieces of paper I pull out of the box admit to wasting or allowing other people to waste for them is over fifty percent of their working day. Some are as high as seventy-five per cent! What was your Waste Factor figure?

If you really want to dramatically improve your results, then one of the first and simplest things you can do is stop wasting time. So here is an exercise for you to do. Complete the two sets of charts on the following pages or reproduce them on other sheets of paper.

The first sheet has two columns headed WAYS I WASTE MY TIME, and HOW I WILL DEAL WITH THIS IN FUTURE.

The second sheet has two columns headed WAYS I ALLOW OTHER PEOPLE TO WASTE MY TIME and HOW I WILL DEAL WITH THIS IN FUTURE.

Complete these sheets.

Ways you waste time could include:

Not having your current day fully planned the day before so you spend time planning it.

The solution could be: I will commit to planning every following day before I leave the office.

Reading an irrelevant magazine.

The solution could be: I will commit to only reading relevant trade magazines in the office and only when I am taking a tea or coffee break.

Shuffling business cards to see whom you could telephone and who you would most like to telephone, instead of calling them all.

The solution could be: Start calling them right away and call them all. If you are never going to call them, dispose of their card so you never shuffle it again.

Making unnecessary telephone calls to kill time.

The solution could be: Commit to never killing time ever again.

Carry on until you have listed every single way that you waste time and how you will not waste it in the future. Then move on to the second sheet.

How you allow others to waste your time could include:

They come over to your desk with a cup of coffee in their hand and want to chat to you while they are drinking it and you are working.

The solution could be: Tell them politely that you have goals you want to achieve today and cannot spare the time.

They come and ask you for advice and say something like, "What would you do in this situation?"

The solution could be that you reply: "Why don't you go and think this through first, come back to me with your solution and I'll see if I agree."

Carry on until you have listed every single way that you allow others to waste your time and how you will not allow them to waste it in the future.

When I carry this exercise out with people in a workshop, the average time they decide they waste shoots up by at least another ten percent. How did you do? How much extra time are you going to have available to you now? How much better will your results be from now on?

Ways I Waste My Time	How I will Deal With This In Future

Ways I Allow Others To Waste My Time	How I Will Deal With This In Future

Technique 2 – The ISWAT Technique

This technique will only work when you have clearly defined goals. If you have them, great! **If you do not, then you need to establish them before this technique will work for you.** Use the Goal Sheet on a following page and complete the three columns. If you don't understand the absolute importance of goal setting, read my book titled 'Smash Your Goals'..

Take a pad of about twenty-five self-adhesive notes and write on them as I have illustrated below. Post them where you are likely to come across them most frequently throughout the day.

> **ISWAT I am
> doing now or
> about to do
> going to help
> me achieve**

Every time you are about to start on a new task or project, READ THE ISWAT NOTE! Ask yourself the question, 'ISWAT I am doing now or about to do going to help me achieve my goal?

If the answer is 'yes', you have three choices. You can do it right away, or you can allocate some specific time to do it later, or you may be fortunate enough to be able to delegate it to someone else, if that is appropriate.

If the answer is 'No – it is not going to help me achieve my goals', you have only one choice – dump it and dump it right away.

If it is another cup of coffee you are going to make – do not make it! If you are going to go and have a chat with a colleague about something unrelated to your goals – do not! If you are about to make a telephone call unrelated to achieving your goals – do not make the call! Invest your time only in what is going to help you to achieve your goals.

GOAL SETTING

Short Term Goals 3-6 months	Medium Term Goals 1-3 years	Ultimate Goal (Just one that summarizes your life's dream)

Cold Calling

5. Researching your prospects

This program is not about marketing, so I'm going to assume that you have already identified your prospects and have a substantial list of these to call, which you will be adding to on a regular basis.

It's very obvious that the more you know about your prospects, the more likely you are to get a positive result when you telephone them. The amount of research you do is dependent on various factors. These include:

- The value of the sale
- The long term value of the customer
- How appropriate the research will be with regard to other prospects operating in the same or similar sectors.

Before we look at what to research before you contact your prospects, let's first take a look at why people are likely to be interested in taking your call and having a conversation with you; in other words 'why people buy'.

Why People Buy

Features and Benefits Don't Sell! My favourite definition of selling which I wrote over twenty years ago is:

'Exposing companies and individuals to problems they never knew they had and to opportunities they never knew existed,

and then showing them how your product or service can solve the problems and exploit the opportunities, and getting them to buy.'

It does NOT say: Exposing companies and individuals to features and benefits!

If you lead with features and benefits, your prospect is most unlikely to be able to relate those to their situation, either because it's not immediately relevant and, more likely, because they have other things on their minds and you haven't caught their interest sufficiently yet.

Yes of course you must know the features and benefits of your product or service – but you talk about those much later in the sales process when you have exposed the problems and opportunities. Let's take this concept a stage further.

People Buy For Emotional Reasons

People buy for emotional reasons and sometimes need logical reasons to justify their decision. Think about some your own buying decisions for a moment. Did you ever go out and buy a new pair of shoes when you had plenty already and your favourite pair just needed new heels, but you bought a new pair anyway because you just love new shoes? Maybe you justified your decision on the basis that if someone saw your bright, shiny, new shoes with the designer name tag, you would create a better impression. Did you ever buy a new car when there was nothing at all wrong with your current model, but the feel and smell of a new car really makes you feel good? Perhaps you justified your decision on the basis that a new, more expensive, luxury car would impress your clients and they would be more likely to do business with you.

I am sure you can think of lots of examples of when you bought something for emotional reasons and then justified them with a logical reason. My own little foible is that I always buy new socks to wear whenever I am speaking at a conference, seminar or workshop. I just love wearing new socks and my logical reason for spending hundreds, if not thousands of pounds a year on new socks, is because they make me feel so good that I believe I will speak much better and therefore attract even more speaking work. I am also a little paranoid that if I do not wear new socks I may not feel so good and may not speak well, which leads me on to the next key point.

People buy for emotional reasons and sometimes need logical reasons to justify their decision and this applies equally in the business to business market as it does the business to consumer market.

The two fundamental emotional buying reasons are TO AVOID PAIN and TO BE HAPPY. Which of those do you think is the greatest buying motivator?

The answer is - **TO AVOID PAIN.**

I will use an analogy to demonstrate this point. Let's suppose that you wake up one morning feeling just a little depressed. You probably do not telephone the doctor, insist on an emergency appointment and demand a prescription for a 'happy pill'. There are many other ways you can cheer yourself up. You can go to a movie, go out for a drink or dinner with some friends, read an amusing book or just get on with the day and put up with a little bit of depression. You know that if you get on with your life the depression will probably soon lift and you will not need to be seeking out a therapist to help you with this.

Compare that situation to waking up one morning with a very bad pain in your head. You take a couple of painkillers but the pain does not go away and, in fact, it gets worse. A half-hour or so later it is so bad that you telephone the doctor for an emergency appointment. When you see them, you literally beg for a prescription for some drug that is going to take this pain away and seek reassurance that there is not something seriously wrong.

Pain is indeed the most powerful motivator, and so, wherever possible, you want to identify where a customer or potential customer is experiencing problems which are giving them pain. Once you have identified those painful situations and shown the customer how you can take the pain away, you are far less likely to get objections to what you are proposing and should have little or no difficulty in making the appointment or closing the sale. In fact the customer should almost be begging to do business with you.

What to research and how to do it

Ideally, you are looking for the following information:

-   General problems that companies in the GENERAL sector you are selling to will be experiencing and that you have been able to solve for similar companies in the past.
-   General problems that companies in the SPECIFIC sector you are selling to will be experiencing and that you have been able to solve for similar companies in the past.
-   Specific problems that companies in the GENERAL sector you are selling to will be experiencing and that you have been able to solve for similar companies in the past.
-   Specific problems that companies in the SPECIFIC sector you are selling to will be experiencing and that you have been able to solve for similar companies in the past.

You are also looking for information as to how you have been able to show your prospect opportunities they maybe were not aware of and how you have been able to help other companies do the same.

Use the sheets on a following page or on separate sheets to compile a list of problems and opportunities you are able to help with in various sectors.

You should know many of these as a result of what you have been able to help customers with in the past. Your colleagues will also have many examples that you may not be aware of. Brainstorm this with them and create a series of case studies, which you can incorporate into your pitch and, later, into your presentation if a meeting will follow.

Where to research

I'm sure I do not have to tell you that the best and easiest form of research that is available to you if you are operating in the business-to-business market, and even to some extent in the business to consumer market is the Internet. When I first started in sales we would have given our right arm to be able to get hold of the information that companies now publish on their websites. What is now available at the click of a mouse would have saved us countless hours of research, frustration and telephone calls.

Your competitors will often have case studies on their websites showing problems they may have been able to solve that hadn't occurred to you. They will often also have them in their brochures and other promotional literature and I'm sure that you could find ways of obtaining copies of this material.

Do you employ someone to set appointments for you?

If you do, don't please fall into the trap of thinking they don't need to know very much and their job is just to make an appointment. They need to know at least half as much as you do, and will know, by the time you have finished this program, if they are going to be making regular appointments for you. If they come across as knowledgeable and don't know the answers to everything they are asked, that's the perfect opportunity for them to say:

"That's a question that's a little out of my depth Mr/ Mrs…… Our sales consultant is the best person to answer that question for you and would have much other important information relative to your situation to show and explain to you. So when could we book in an appointment for them to see you please? I know Mark has a free slot on Tuesday at 11.am and Thursday at 3pm. Which of those is good for you?"

Cold Calling

BUSINESS SECTOR	PROBLEM	OPPORTUNITY

www.bruceking.co.uk

6. Preparing your approach

Let's discuss 'scripts' first of all, because I know that 'script' is a word and a concept that a lot of people react badly to when I tell them to write one.

William Shakespeare wrote: 'All the world's a stage and each must play a part'. Of course he wasn't referring specifically to salespeople when he wrote that – but in my book, it's very relevant indeed.

Imagine the scene. The Globe theatre is packed with an audience eagerly anticipating the production of The Merchant of Venice. Meanwhile, behind the curtains, a group of actors are in quiet discussion.

"Anyone ever done the Merchant of Venice before?" asks one.

"No but I've got a vague idea of how it goes" says another.

"Can't be that difficult. I'm sure we'll wing our way through it OK" says another.

"Let's face it, the audience won't know if we got it a little wrong anyway" says another.

And so they go on stage, not ever having studied the script, totally unprepared – **and it's a mess!**

Of course that would not happen. So why would any salesperson not know precisely what they are going to say during a telephone call or a sales presentation? Why would they not know what questions they were going to ask? Why would they not know all the questions they were likely to be asked and have answers prepared? Why, why, why would they not have a script to work to and rehearse, rehearse, rehearse? Let's face it – when we are selling, we're on stage! And the larger the value of the sale and / or the long term value of the customer or client – the more rehearsals are needed.

The purpose of writing a script is NOT to follow it word for word and refuse to be sidetracked. The purpose is:

- To know precisely what you are going to say in your opening statement to arouse interest and to get the prospect to want to continue with A CONVERSATION.
- To have answers to all the questions that you know, from your experience and the experience of others, are likely to be asked during that CONVERSATION and know how to respond effectively so the prospect wants to continue with the CONVERSATION and ultimately agree to your proposal.

The only difference between a salesperson on the telephone and an actor on stage is that the actor cannot walk on stage with their script. They have to learn it off by heart. When you are selling a product, service or appointment on the telephone, you have the advantage that you can keep your script or the key points from your script nearby to refer to. Not so in face to face presentations!

Only when you have written the near perfect script and know each section of it off by heart can you relax and have a CONVERSATION knowing you can handle just about everything that comes up during that conversation. So let's look at how best to structure your opening statement and you can tailor these approaches and the follow up, whether you are calling to make an appointment or to sell your product or service over the telephone.

You'll notice I've emphasized the word 'conversation' frequently. Now let me expand upon this…

I mentioned earlier in this program that we've all been on the receiving end of numerous dreadful cold calls and the last thing you want is to appear to be from the same mould. The impression you want to give as fast as you possibly can is that you are pleasant, knowledgeable, and could be a trusted advisor and an asset to their business – even if you are simply selling toilet paper. And that was meant with the greatest of respect to janitorial suppliers. My own supplier knows more about Health & Safety issues than most others I've met – she's a trusted advisor!

In order to come across that way, you must have a professional, enthusiastic but relaxed approach; engage the prospect's interest as quickly as possible by appearing knowledgeable and an authority on your subject; and engage them in a **conversation** as quickly as possible that will enhance your reputation with them and put you head and shoulders above your competition.

Having said that, I should also emphasize that you are not setting yourself up or should not be allowing yourself to be set up to be intimidated, pushed around or used as an unpaid consultant by the prospect. Indeed the opposite applies. As an expert in your field, you deserve and should expect respect. Arrogance on your part is of course not acceptable, BUT let me assure you that the most successful salespeople I know are just a tiny bit South of arrogant!

So a word of caution here, and meant with the greatest of respect to you as well. If you are not an expert in your field, then you owe it to yourself and your prospects to become an expert as fast as you possibly can! Do what is necessary to justify that qualification - FAST!

Have a goal for a call

As in life – as in cold calling. If you are going to get what you want, you need to know what you want. When it comes to cold calling, it's absolutely essential to have a clear intention for what you want the ideal result of the call to be. Without that, you cannot possibly frame the correct questions that will get you that result. You should also have a satisfactory fallback position so you get something out of the call that will leave you in a positive frame of mind. The result you want could be one or more of the following:

- Establish there is or is not a need for your product or service

- Establish who is the person you need to be speaking with

- Establish when they will be available

- Make a sale

- Make an appointment

- Get an agreement to talk them through an online presentation or webinar

- Get an agreement they will visit your website and when to call back

- Get an agreement that literature or other information can be sent and when you can call back for a review

Do you have anything to add to that list?

Your opening statement of question

How NOT to start a conversation

These are things you should NEVER say:

"How are you today?"

"I'm sorry to bother you but…"

"I'm sorry to trouble you but"

"Do you have a minute to talk right now?"

"Am I interrupting?"

"Have you heard of us?"

"This is NOT a sales call"

Those may have made you aware of some other 'no-no' opening statements you use as well. If it has – don't use those either.

Effective opening statements

Here are a few examples of good opening statements. They are varied in style and approach and, later in the program, we'll extend some of these into the actual conversations that followed:

To find out if someone might be experiencing a particular problem:

"Good morning John, it's Bruce King calling from the XYZ Company. I'm working with a few other companies in your sector, most of who seem to be experiencing the same challenges in particular areas of their business. So the reason

I'm calling you is to ask if you're open to having a brief chat to see if you're experiencing similar problems, and if so how we might help- you too.   Would that be OK?"

Referred as someone who might be experiencing a particular problem:

"Good morning John, it's Bruce King calling. I believe Robert Smith of The Board Company Limited told you to expect my call. Robert mentioned that a particular situation, which concerned another Sales Director of a large organization in a similar business sector to your own, might be of interest to you. Do you have just a few moments to speak right now?

To someone who might benefit from an opportunity:

"Good morning John, it's Jason Smith calling from the XYZ Company. I'm working with a few other companies in your sector, and I've been able to provide them with a simple system that has increased the amount of sales calls their reps are making by up to 77%, with a corresponding increase in sales. So the reason I'm calling you is to ask if you're open to having a brief chat right now to see if that 's something you'd be interested in exploring in some more detail.   Would that be OK?"

Short and starts with a question almost immediately:

I'm a salesperson approach – direct and to the point with a clever twist:

"Good morning Peter. I'm Bruce King from Bruce King & Associates and this is a sales call; probably the last thing you need right now, so can I just take 45 seconds to tell you what I do and then you can decide if you want to take another two or three minutes on the phone or hang up. Is that fair? (Yes).

Thank you. I help companies whose sales teams are struggling to meet their sales targets to meet or exceed them in a very short space of time. My question is: what are some of the things you'd want to know before being comfortable to invite me in for a face to face meeting?"

Shortly after they start to speak, you interrupt and say:

"Excuse me interrupting Peter but I have a challenge here. I did say 45 seconds and that's up. Are you sure you want to continue?"

Brief, polite and questioning:

"Good morning Susan, this is Sharon Michaels from the XYZ company. I'm working with a number of other accountants in your area and I'm calling to ask if you're open to discussing a more cost effective and efficient way of handling the storage of client's files. I was hoping we could ask each other a few questions to see if it's worth spending some more time discussing this at a later date? Would that be OK please?"

Write some opening statements that you plan to use from now on, either below or on separate sheets.

My Opening Statements

---

7. The conversation

By now, you are almost certainly seeing how several different approaches can achieve the same desired result – a conversation. So now let's take two of these examples and go through the entire presentation. Bear in mind that the salesperson has gone through all the necessary preparatory work and from this point on, is no longer working from a script word for word. Instead they are using all their knowledge and skills to have a conversation.

In this first example, the prospect is a referral and has a problem. All the salesperson has to do is act very professionally and aim to get the appointment as quickly as possible with the least amount of pressure on the prospect.

Salesperson: *"Good morning John, it's Bruce King calling. I believe Robert Smith of The Board Company Limited told you to expect my call. Robert mentioned that a particular situation, which concerned another Sales Director of a large organization in a similar business sector to your own, might be of interest to you. Do you have a few moments right now?"*

Prospect: *"Yes – Robert did mention you when I met him last night, so carry on."*

Salesperson *"Thank you. The issue this organization had and that Robert thought might interest you was that their salespeople were spending too much time taking orders from existing customers and were not opening enough new* accounts. *Customers were required to place all orders, including repeat business through the salesperson, leaving them insufficient time for developing new business. Is that a situation you might also be experiencing?"*

Prospect: *"I am having some concerns in that area. What precisely did you have in mind?"*

Salesperson: *"Thank you for confirming that. What happened in that case was we made a detailed study of their current methodology and came up with three ways to maximize the time a salesperson had to spend generating new business through more effective prospecting and referral systems AND ways to motivate them to achieve their targets for new business. We helped them develop some relatively simple internal systems for achieving this and developed a training system for the sales team. The result was that over the following six months, the customer base increased by twenty-three percent and sales increased by thirty eight percent. Would that kind of result impress you?"*

Prospect: *"It couldn't fail to could it. Of course budgets are tight right now so a lot would depend upon the cost and whether or not you could achieve the same result for us."*

Salesperson: *"At this stage, I really couldn't say. We have achieved the same results – and better - with similar organizations to yours but I'd need to know a lot more about your business before I could be certain. What I would like to do, if it's OK with you, is meet with you in person, discuss your* situation in a lot more detail and then we'd both be a lot clearer as to what could be achieved. When could we arrange that – what slots do you have in your diary next week?"

In this next example, the salesperson has three 'pains' ready to mention which are specific to the business sector the prospect operates in.

Salesperson: *"Good morning John, it's Bruce King calling. Thanks for taking my call. I'm working with a number of other companies operating in your business sector who have all been experiencing significant problems in three areas of their business. Do you have a few moments right now for me to tell you what they are and for us to ask each other a few questions to see if it's worth continuing with this conversation?.*

Prospect: *"I've got a couple of minutes at most."*

Salesperson *"Thank you. There are three main areas they are having difficulty with:*

1: Sales team are not meeting targets for generating new customers

2: Sales team are spending too much time taking small orders from existing customers which are not contributing sufficiently to their overall sales targets

3: Because of this, the sales managers and the sales team are frustrated and de-motivated.

Can you relate to any of these issues?"

Prospect: *"I certainly have some concerns in two of those areas. What precisely did you have in mind?"*

Salesperson: *"Can you tell me more specifically about those two situations and how they are affecting your business? Naturally it's totally confidential."*

A conversation develops culminating in a request from the prospect: *"So what can you do for us?"*

Salesperson: *I've no idea right now John. What happened in one of the situations I was involved in is that we made a detailed study of their current methodology and came up with three ways to maximize the time a salesperson had to spend generating new business through more effective prospecting and referral systems AND ways to motivate them to achieve their targets for new business. We helped them develop some relatively simple internal systems for achieving this and developed a training system for the sales team. The result was that over the following six months, the customer base increased by twenty-three percent and sales increased by thirty eight percent. Would that kind of result impress you?"*

Prospect: *"It couldn't fail to could it. Of course budgets are tight right now so a lot would depend upon the cost and whether or not you could achieve the same result for us."*

Salesperson: *"At this stage, I really couldn't say. We have achieved the same results – and better with similar organizations to yours but I'd need to know a lot more about your business before I could be certain. What I would like to do, if it's OK with you, is meet with you in person, discuss your situation in a lot more detail and then we'd both be a lot clearer as to what could be achieved. When could we arrange that – what slots do you have in your diary next week?"*

In this next example, the prospect is a cold call and was initially very resistant. The salesperson could easily have given in at any stage of this call but used questioning skills and objection handling skills to create the opportunity to close on an appointment in the subsequent call. Also note that she asked for referrals at the end of the conversation!

Prospect: *"John Smith speaking".*

Mary: *"Good morning John. My name is Mary Wilson from Abbey Office Furniture. I understand you are the person who deals with purchasing office furniture. Is that correct?"*

Prospect: *"Yes but we don't need anything right now. Call me again in six months and I may discuss it then."*

Mary: *"I understand and I appreciate your honesty. John, I'm calling because Abbey Office Furniture would like to be the company you look to when you do have a need for furniture. Our customers love our mix of quality, design and competitive pricing. Could you please tell me how we could position ourselves to earn the opportunity to be considered?"*

Prospect: *"Top of the list would be pricing. You'd have to be able to offer the most competitive prices. Why don't you just put a catalogue and price list in the post?"*

Mary: *"John, let's assume we could offer you the lowest or, at very least, most competitive pricing. What other factors would be strongly considered before you decided who you would place a future order with?"*

Prospect: *"Mary, just send me some information in the mail."*

Mary: *"I'd be very happy to do that John. I have a tremendous amount of different literature here, some of which may not be of any interest to you. Do you mind if I ask you a few questions so I can just send what I believe will be relevant?"*

Prospect: *"Go on then."*

Mary: *"Thank you. When do you anticipate you might need to invest in more furniture and is there a particular project you have in mind?"*

Prospect: *"We'll be fitting out a new tele-sales department for twenty operators in about nine months time."*

At this point Mary asked a series of questions relating to the type of layout they were anticipating and the type of furniture required. Then:

Mary: *"John, I'm going to put some brochures together today. May I make an appointment to bring them round and go through the information with you? Can we organize that?"*

Prospect: *"No. Just put them in the post."*

Mary: *"OK. I'll do that. How long do you need to review what I send you?"*

Prospect: *"Forty-eight hours I suppose."*

Mary: *"OK, so I'll call you on Monday and here is what I would like to happen. If you are comfortable with this approach, I'd like you to say that you have read through the brochures and particularly my notes on our free design service and there's absolutely no reason for us to meet. OR you can tell me that there is some interest, in which case I'd like you to call me in for a face-to-face meeting. Is that fair John?"*

Prospect: *"Very fair indeed Mary."*

Mary: *"Thank you. You have a lovely week-end and we'll speak on Monday. Just one more thing before I hang up John. I like to spend most of my time looking after my clients, not looking for them. So I'd really appreciate your help please. I believe there are several other offices on your business park and when I come to see you, I'd love to be able to drop in and introduce myself to two or three other organizations while I'm there. Who are your nearest neighbours?"*

Prospect: *"The only ones that spring to mind are Acme and Trident. You could call them."*

Mary: *"Thanks for that. Would you by any chance know the names of the people I should be speaking to there?"*

Prospect: *"Joe Johnson at Acme but I don't know who at Trident."*

Mary: *"Thank you so much for that. We'll speak on Monday. Goodbye."*

Prospect: *"Goodbye. I look forward to your call."*

On the following page, or on a separate sheet or sheets of paper, write the key points that you simply must bring up in your conversation and some questions that will enable you to do so.

KEY POINTS	QUESTIONS TO ASK

Cold Calling

8. How to handle 'gatekeepers'

Of course you're not always going to get put through immediately to the person you want to speak with. Most of your prospects will have someone in place to protect them from cold calls and so a great deal of your success is going to depend upon how you deal with the gatekeepers.

The first thing to understand is that the gatekeeper is not a nasty, snarling, ill-tempered, difficult person, hired only for their ability to destroy the confidence and livelihoods of salespeople who cold call. They are usually very pleasant, competent people with a variety of other responsibilities, and they would not have their jobs if they were not pleasant and competent. It's just that one of their roles is to prevent their boss from being constantly interrupted by cold calls from people they have no interest in talking to. Their job is to screen calls and only put those through that they are convinced could be of interest to the boss.

So don't start off on the wrong foot and expect them to be horrible to you – because what you think is what you get - most of the time! And change your attitude to them entirely.

From now on think of them as 'door openers'.

The first rule of dealing with door openers is to be pleasant, professional and friendly. You want to make them your friend – or at least not alienate them from the moment you start to speak. That does not however mean groveling or being over friendly and gushing!

Here are some examples of effective ways to negotiate with the door opener, starting with a very different approach, which I call **'The Reverse Questioning Technique'.**

Door openers are taught to ask you four questions:

Who are you?

What company do you represent?

Are they expecting your call?

What's it in connection with?

I bet you've heard those before.

And once they start that, for you it becomes a tap dance. You have to try to dance your way around those questions – or answer them – practiced and perfectly. But let me share with you just one strategy I use that gets me through 87% of the time, if the person I am calling for is in.

Instead of allowing them to ask you questions, you ask them questions. It is something they are so Not used to, that you take control.

It goes like this:

They answer the telephone and the first thing you say is…

- Who am I speaking with? So now you have their name, let's say it's Joan. Then you ask

- Max Jones isn't in is he Joan? And if Max is in, they'll likely say – 'mmm yes he is'. Then you ask:

- But he's just gone into a meeting hasn't he Joan? And if he hasn't – they'll say NO. So then you ask:

- So he's just taken another call? And if he has not, they'll say NO and you say:

- Great – I'll take him Joan – it's Bruce King.

It needs a little practice to become totally confident and come across positively. But it works. It works for me, and thousands of other people I've taught it to. It will work for you too.

Here are some other, more traditional and effective ways to work with the door opener and get their cooperation:

"John Smith please" (Puts you through)

"Is John in"?

"Who's that?"

"Bruce King - can you put me through to John please." (Puts you through)

Cold Calling

"John Smith please"

"Who's speaking?"

"Bruce King - can you put me through to John please."

"Does he know you?"

"Yes he does" (He doesn't – but never mind)

(Puts you through)

"John Smith please"

"Who's speaking?"

"Bruce King – who am I speaking with please?"

"I'm Mary – John's PA"

"Hello Mary - can you put me through to John please."

"Does he know you?"

"Yes" (He doesn't – but never mind)

"What company are you from?"

"Bruce King & Associates"   (Puts you through)

"John Smith please"

"Who's speaking?"

"Bruce King – who am I speaking with please?"

"I'm Mary – John's PA"

"Hello Mary - can you put me through to John please."

"Does he know you?"

"Yes" (He doesn't – but never mind)

"What company are you from?"

"Bruce King & Associates"

"And what's it in connection with?"

Now there are several approaches you can take from here. For example:

"Robert from the XYZ Company recommended I call and he is expecting me."

"I'm working with a few other companies in your sector, and I've been able to provide them with a simple system that has increased the amount of sales calls their reps are making by up to 77%, with a corresponding increase in sales. It's something I'm sure John would want to know about, so can you put me through please Mary."

"He wanted me to call him a few days after I sent him some suggestions/proposals/confidential information and he would have received that three days ago. So can you put me through please Mary." (your letter may have had a PS: I will call you in a few days time unless I hear from your PA that you have no interest.)

"I have some information for him about some of the problems his competitors are having and which I'm sure he'd like to know about. So can you put me through please Mary."

Another completely different approach you can build in anywhere through any of these conversations if you are having difficulty getting through with any of these approaches, is to throw the door opener off balance. They basically have four questions they are trained to ask you. These are:

Asking them questions that don't fit into that framework can disarm them. So ask questions or respond to questions like this:

"What's it about?"

"I'd be happy to tell you Mary but it's important I speak with him directly"

"What's it about?"

"I'm not really sure, which is why I need to speak to John"

"What are you selling?"

"I don't understand"

"What are you selling?"

"Does John want to sell something to me?"

"What's the weather like there Mary?"

"Is this going to take long Mary, because I'm calling long distance?"

"What else do you need to know about me personally before you put me through Mary?"

"Mary, if you were me, and you had some really important information for John and a couple of questions for him, what would you do?"

And as a last resort:

"What are you hoping to achieve by not putting me through to John?"

"Are you willing to risk your company losing a lot of money by not putting my call through?"

"OK, in that case may I please take your full name so that when somebody from your organization complains to my boss they didn't get to speak with me, I can give them the contact I did speak to?"

Voicemail

How many times have you either fought your way past the door opener, or been so happy to have been put through right away, only to be on the receiving end of a voicemail message? Quite often, no doubt. And how many times did you either just hang up or leave a garbled message because you simply weren't prepared?

Here are three ways to deal with voicemail:

1: Have three 'pains' specific to the prospect's sector ready. These would be the same three you were going to discuss at some point in your conversation anyway. Your message is therefore:

"There are three reasons why you should return my call. (give the three reasons). My name is XXXX from XXXXX Company and my number is XXXX. I look forward to your call, thank you."

2: *"Deleting this message won't get rid of the three main problems most businesses in your sector are suffering. So please call me back. My name is XXXX from XXXXX Company and my number is XXXX. I look forward to your call, thank you."*

3: *My name is XXXX from XXXXX Company and my number is XXXX. There are three main problems most businesses in your sector are suffering right now. They are one, XXXXXXXXXXXX, two XXXXXXX* **BUT** *half way through explaining the second one you hang up as if the call was cut off.*

On the following pages or on separate sheets, write some examples of voice mail messages you will leave in the future.

VOICE MAIL MESSAGES

Cold Calling

www.bruceking.co.uk

9. Handling objections

No matter how well prepared you are and how much you have rehearsed your opening statement and content of your conversations, things will not always go as smoothly as you would like. Go back to the conversation earlier in this program where Mary from the office furniture company was engaged in a conversation with her prospect. Objections came up throughout and Mary handled them well and achieved most of her goals. So let's spend some time now dealing with how to handle objections.

I have heard some sales trainers describe an objection as merely a request for further information. Frankly, I think this is nonsense. The dictionary definition of objection is *'an expression, statement or feeling of opposition or dislike'*. My thesaurus lists the following words as suitable alternatives: *censure, counter-argument, doubt, exception, niggle, protest and opposition*. How, therefore, could anyone describe an objection as a request for further information? That type of attitude to what is often a genuine initial rejection of your proposals inevitably leads to failure to secure an order. Fortunately, the psychology for handling objections is not difficult to understand.

The three types of objections

There are three basic types of objections. These are imagined objections, pretend objections and valid objections. Let's take a closer look at these.

Imagined Objections

The imagined objection is just that – a figment of your prospect's imagination. The following are typical examples of imagined objections:

-   We couldn't afford it.

-   I couldn't afford the running costs of this car; it's probably too heavy on fuel.

-   I don't know if my wife would like it.

-   I don't think it would fit.

-   I don't think this carpet will match my curtains.

-   I don't think I could get the board to agree

Now look at these statements again with my comments in brackets. It will be obvious that these are all imagined objections.

"We couldn't afford it." [Your prospect does not know the cost or what credit terms are available.]

"I couldn't afford the running costs of this car; it's probably too heavy on fuel." [They do not yet know that although the engine is larger, the new, improved fuel injection system increases fuel economy by 25 per cent.]

"I don't know if my wife would like it." [He hasn't asked her yet.]

"I don't think it would fit." [She hasn't measured it yet.]

"I don't think this carpet will match my curtains." [He has not yet seen them together.]

"I don't think I could get the board to agree." [He has not asked them yet.]

Pretend Objections

What about pretend objections? Probably the most frequent pretend objection you get is when a prospect claims to be too busy to see you. How many times has that been said to you? It is obviously a pretend objection. If I were to telephone you and told you that you had just won the Lottery, that I had a cheque for you for five million pounds and just needed fifteen minutes with you to complete the paperwork and give you the money, would you find the time in your very busy schedule to see me?

Other frequent pretend objections include:

- We cannot afford it

- It's not in the budget

- I don't have the authority to make the decision

Valid Objections

Valid objections are just what the title suggests. They are legitimate and real reasons why people may not be able to purchase your product or service from you and therefore are likely to be the most difficult to deal with. Nevertheless, you can deal with them on most occasions.

Having spent many years teaching thousands of people to sell a huge variety of products and services, it has become apparent to me it is very rare indeed that more than six valid objections can be made against any particular product or service.

It is essential to know all the imagined, pretend and valid objections that can be leveled against what you are selling, and to rehearse responses to them. This is therefore a further exercise for you to carry out, and as I often find what one person in a company's sales force is finding difficulty dealing with, another finds very easy, this is again an exercise you should brainstorm with your colleagues.

The basic rules for handling objections

Before dealing with the basic rules for handling objections, I am going to introduce another concept which really falls under the heading of 'closing techniques', but which needs to be discussed now because you will use it frequently when handling objections and, indeed, when presenting your opening statement and during your conversation..

The Silent Close

When I mention the term 'closing question', you need to be aware that I am referring to any question that moves you on to the next stage of the sales process. So for example – "can you put me through to John please?" is a closing question.

The golden rule is: **whenever you ask a closing question, keep quiet!** The first person to speak will almost certainly be the loser. If it is your prospect, he or she either has to say 'yes' to your proposition or raise another objection to going ahead. It will almost certainly be an objection that you can deal with. If you speak first, the pressure is off the prospect and back on you. You will have to spend a lot more time trying to regain control of the situation.

A little while ago I was negotiating with a large organization who were considering my proposals for a sales training contract. This was the second meeting with the company. The first had been with the sales director and now I was meeting with the CEO. As far as I was concerned, this was going to be a closing meeting. I'm sure you also realize that when you are selling sales training services, you had better be good and be able to demonstrate what you are going to teach.

I sat opposite the CEO and went through my proposals with him. I summarized the problems the company had been experiencing with their sales teams. I summarized my solutions and asked if he was as certain as his sales director that my solutions would solve the problems. His response was *"I think they will Bruce"*. I then asked one of my favourite closing questions: **"so where do we go from here*?"** and shut up!

There was a silence of about ten seconds and then a bright neon sign lit up on the CEO's forehead. It said 'He's using the silent close on me'. I smiled and a neon sign lit up on my forehead, which said 'I know you know'. So we sat facing each other, smiling and maintaining eye contact except for my deliberate glance at his office clock from time to time.

After eleven minutes and fifteen seconds he burst out laughing and said *"I just wanted to see how long you were going to keep that up for Bruce"*, to which my response was *"so will I be starting April or May?"* (Alternative question close followed by silent close). Five seconds later he responded *"April"*.

So remember the silent close – the first person to speak loses most of the time. AND it is equally effective when used over the telephone.

Before dealing with some common and specific objections, let us first take a look at the basic techniques for handling all objections.

1 - Respect imagined and pretend objections

The most fundamental principle you must come to terms with when dealing with objections of any kind, is never to argue and never to let the experience of handling an objection develop into a confrontation. Whilst you may know that an objection is either imagined or pretend, you must always treat it as if it were valid. Nobody likes to be ignored or treated as if they were foolish and dealing with every type of objection as if it were a valid one will gain you the respect, trust and friendship of your prospect.

2 – Acknowledge the objection before responding

Whenever you are responding to an objection, always start by acknowledging it. It tells the prospect you have heard and accept what they have said. For example, when the prospect says to you, *"It's more than we wanted to pay Bruce"*, you start your response *with "I appreciate it's more than you wanted to pay Phil, and …* (your response)."

Not only does this tell them that you are listening, but because you are mirroring their speech, it is also telling their subconscious mind that you are just like them, they like you, can trust you and would like to do business with you.

3 – Listen and let them finish

When I am presenting at a conference or workshop, I ask the attendees to raise their hands if they like to be interrupted when they are speaking. Not a single hand ever goes up. Then I ask how many of them interrupt other people when they are speaking. A sea of hands arises. Do you interrupt prospects when they are raising an objection or asking a question and taking rather a long time in doing so? I'll guess you do.

Why would you do this? You invest time in finding the prospect, researching their background, making the initial contact and securing an appointment. You invest time establishing a good rapport, asking questions and then presenting how your product or service can help them solve their problems and remove their pain. You invest a lot of time and effort in your prospect. So why, when they raise an objection or ask a question, do you interrupt them and risk ruining the relationship and losing the sale when you were so close to getting the result you wanted. Nobody wants to do business with people who interrupt them.

From now on, no matter how many times you have heard the question or objection before, listen and let them finish. No matter how bored you are of hearing the same old thing time after time, you must look interested, nod, smile and let them know you are taking them seriously. Then use the 'Pause, Think, Respond' technique.

Even if you know the answer to it because you have heard the question many times before, do not immediately blurt the answer out. PAUSE and look as if you are taking the question very seriously and are THINKING about it. Whether it is an imagined, pretend or valid objection, your prospect needs to know you are taking it seriously. Then you can RESPOND.

4 – Ask them to elaborate

Sometimes prospects will have a genuine objection, but because they feel under pressure or are just not good at phrasing what they are thinking in a clear and concise manner, what they say is not necessarily what they mean. Ask them to elaborate, posing questions such as *"I don't understand, can you explain that to me?"* or *"What do you mean exactly?"*, or "that's interesting – tell me more", followed by the Silent Close.

Asking them to elaborate, rather than coming back with an immediate response, achieves a number of things.

- It gives them a little more time and takes the pressure off them

- It will give you a clearer understanding of their concern

- It makes them feel they are maybe a little smarter than you and therefore less threatened

That last point is particularly important. Whilst prospects want to deal with intelligent and professional people who are going to provide the highest quality of service to them, they can also be a little wary of people they think may be much smarter than they are. Asking them to elaborate therefore often makes them feel more comfortable with you.

The other major advantage in asking a prospect to elaborate on an objection is that in many cases he or she will talk themselves out of it without you having to say anything. This is particularly true of the imagined or pretend objection. Many times I have asked a prospect to elaborate and, after a lengthy silence and possibly some waffled explanation, they have agreed, without any prompting from me, that the objection was in fact invalid.

5 – Identify all the real objections

When a prospect feels under pressure or a little unsure, they will often stall the process by blurting out the first thing that comes to mind. If you respond promptly and satisfactorily to the first, they will just raise another. Therefore the technique you should use is to get all of the objections out in the open before responding to any of them. Very often it is only the last one that is, in fact, a genuine objection.

When the first objection is raised, you say: "Just supposing we could get around that" or, "Just supposing that wasn't an issue, is there anything else that is stopping you from going ahead?" (Silent Close).

If they raise another objection, you repeat that same question and keep doing that until all their objections are out in the open and they say "No – nothing else."

Then you ask, *"So if I can satisfy you one hundred percent on each of those points, will you be going ahead?"* (Silent Close).

If the response to that is "No", or they seem unsure, you still have not got all of the objections out in the open and need to ask again *"'What else would be stopping you going ahead then?"*

If the answer is "Yes", only then do you answer the objections.

6 – Confirm they are no longer an Objection

Once you have answered an objection it is absolutely essential that you get your prospect's agreement that it no longer exists. Do not assume that because you have answered it to your satisfaction you have answered it to theirs. Ask *"Have I covered that to your satisfaction?"* (Silent Close), or *"Are you now satisfied completely on that point?"* (Silent Close), or *"Is there anything else you need to know on that subject before I continue?"* (Silent Close).

Getting your prospect's confirmation that the objection no longer exists removes the likelihood of them raising it again when you are asking for the sale. An objection that has not been satisfactorily answered and confirmed as no longer relevant by your prospect, can always be brought up again.

7 – Replace 'But' and 'However' with 'AND'

Having listened to thousands of salespeople answering objections, I know that you too often use the words 'but' and 'however'. For example, your prospects says to you, *"It's more than we wanted to pay"* and you respond *"'I appreciate it's more than you wanted to pay Phil BUT (or HOWEVER), let me run through the figures again and show you why it's going to give you such an excellent return on your investment."*

Make no mistake about this, the words 'but' and 'however' are argumentative. You are effectively telling the prospect that they are wrong and you are right. On a conscious and subconscious level, you are raising a potentially insurmountable barrier between you and your prospect. You have possibly lost more business through using these words than anything else you could have done or said. In future, replace the words 'but' and 'however' with AND. Always remember that 'but' and 'however' separate people. The word 'AND' joins people together.

For example:

"It's more than we wanted to pay Bruce."

"I appreciate it's more than you wanted to pay Phil AND let me run through the figures again and show you why it's going to give you such an excellent return on your investment."

Do you see how much more effective this is going to be?

8 – Feel, Felt, Found

The feel, felt, found technique works so well with every prospect. Here is an example of what you would say, tailored of course to your specific product or service.

"I understand exactly how you FEEL John. Many of our clients FELT exactly the same way when we first presented this solution to them. And what they FOUND was that their return on investment was far better than they had expected and they have all become long term clients of ours."

Now look at the structure of that paragraph:

'I understand exactly how you FEEL'. This demonstrates that you empathize with their concern, that you understand them and are on their side.

'Many of our clients FELT exactly the same way...' demonstrates that it is quite all right for them to feel that way and that there is nothing unusual about how they feel.

"And what they FOUND was..." demonstrates the benefits your other clients received as a result of their purchase.

Now let us take a look at some specific objections or stalls and the ones you are likely to come across most frequently.

I'm happy with our current supplier

Probably the most frequent objection that most salespeople come up with unless they have a new, unique product or service that has never been seen or heard of before. So when you hear "I'm happy with our current supplier", you can use any of the following:

"I'm sure you are John otherwise you wouldn't be doing business with them. What do you like about them most of all?"

(Response).

"And is there anything at all you'd like them to improve on?"

"I appreciate you're happy with them John. Does that mean you've made a firm decision never to talk to another potential supplier ever again for any reason?"

And in response to a similar statement such as *"I doubt you could do better than / beat our current suppliers"*...

You ask: *"What does do better / beat look like to you?"*

Price objections

If there is one thing for certain that every prospect will try to negotiate on, it is price and price objections can be presented to you in a number of ways. A common statement voiced by a prospect will be "It's too expensive". Note I used the word 'statement'. They did not ask a question such as "How much can you reduce it by?" They just made a statement. Therefore, even if you have the authority to reduce your price, this is not the time to start thinking about doing so.

The statement *'It's too expensive'*, should be responded to with a question from you, that should be either "Which means?" (Silent Close) or "So where do we go from here?" (Silent Close). In using either of these responses, you are passing the decision on what to do back to your prospect, which serves two purposes. Firstly, it makes them think they are in control because you have given them a choice and, secondly, and more importantly, it means they have to make the next move.

I used this technique with a prospect just a few weeks ago when I quoted them my highest price ever for a five-day conference tour in India. When I asked him *"So where do we go from here Ramin?"* (Silent Close), I was met with a slight pause, followed by the response *"I suppose we'll have to increase the ticket price a little then"*. Therefore, whenever you are faced with a price objection, do not automatically start thinking of reducing your price. There may be many other ways the prospect can meet your quoted price.

The prospect may come back with the same price objection, perhaps worded slightly differently, such as in "It's definitely more than we want to spend". You could respond to this second price objection with the question "That's not unusual. Off the record, in round numbers, what price were you hoping for?" (Silent Close).

Of course it is not 'off the record', but a prospect's subconscious mind hears those words and associates them with genuinely being 'off the record'. This, combined with the words 'round numbers', puts the prospect off guard and they are then much more likely to tell you what they were actually hoping to pay, and are prepared to pay, rather than giving you a price way below as would often happen in a price negotiation. Another way of identifying what their price point is could be to ask the question: "In round numbers, off the record, how much too much is it?" (Silent Close).

I have to discuss it with….

Sometimes you may forget to establish early on in your conversation that the person you are speaking with has the authority to purchase. Other times, in spite of the fact that they had told you they do have the authority, they will still use the classic stall – "I have to discuss it with…." Now here is the challenge. They are either telling the truth or they are not, and you do not know which is correct.

If they had told you earlier that they had the authority to purchase then your response to this stall should simply be, "That is not what you told me earlier. Why have you changed your mind?" (Silent Close). Yes - that may appear confrontational, but said quietly and pleasantly, it does not need to sound that way. They either told you a lie or they have changed the terms you agreed to, so you are perfectly entitled to ask that question and expect an answer.

If they had not told you that they had the authority because you forgot to ask, or they are adamant that, in spite of the fact they had, they still have to discuss it with someone else, you then ask "Would you like to go ahead and will you be recommending you do?" (Silent Close).

If they seem unsure or say "No", then you have not sold them on your product or service. They still have concerns that need addressing and it is now up to you to start questioning again to identify the reasons why. When you have done that satisfactorily, you may well find that they no longer have to discuss it with anyone and that they were simply using that as an excuse because they were not convinced. If you had not asked that question, it is almost certain you would have lost the sale.

If, on the other hand, they say "Yes", then you need to ask a number of other questions. These could include:

"Would you like me to present our proposals with you?" (Silent Close).

If you cannot attend the meeting, then ask:

"What help, information or other materials do you need from me in order to present this to them so they agree?" (Silent Close).

If they genuinely want to recommend they go ahead, you need to ensure as far as possible that they present your proposal in the best way available and have all the supporting materials required to do so.

I want to think about it

It is estimated that when someone says they "want to think it over", in ninety-seven out of one hundred cases, they will not and you will not get the sale. Yes, you may get the remaining three out of the hundred, but with those odds I would far sooner you had a "no" and moved on to a new prospect than sat at home after a hard day's work believing you had all those prospects thinking your proposal over. So here is an example of how do deal with 'I want to think it over':

You: *I appreciate you may want to think about it. Generally speaking, when a client says something like that to me, it means I haven't explained something properly. So please tell me - what is it I've not made clear - is it the (name any one feature of your product or service that you think may have caused the objection e.g. cost/size/service intervals)?* (Silent Close).

Prospect: *It's the cost of it.*

You: *I can understand that cost may be an issue. In addition to that, is there anything else that's stopping you from going ahead?* (Silent Close).

Prospect: *No.*

You: *So if we can deal satisfactorily with the investment required, is there any reason why we couldn't go ahead today?* (Silent Close).

Prospect: *No.*

The more pain you can expose and the more your prospect is hurting thinking about their problems or lack of opportunities, the less likely a prospect is to raise objections. Nevertheless, objections will come up from time to time and the more effectively you can handle them using these techniques, the easier it will become to make a sale or an appointment.

On the following page or separate sheets, list all the objections you must frequently encounter and how you will respond to them in the future.

OBJECTION	RESPONSE

www.bruceking.co.uk

10. Asking for the appointment & closing the sale

I hear a lot of sales trainers and salespeople complain about the use of the term 'closing a sale'. One of the criticisms often voiced is that the word 'close' relates to the end of something, whereas getting a sale from a customer should be the 'start' of a relationship. Others feel it is too harsh a word and reflects badly on their professionalism. Well I say 'phooey'!

The term 'close the sale' is brief, to the point, and we all know what it means. It means getting an order or an agreement to move on to the next stage in the buying process. Selling is the oldest profession and the term 'close the sale' has been used for hundreds of years and will probably be used for many hundreds more to come. And here's the truth of the matter; if you don't ask for the sale and instead, wait for the prospect to volunteer to buy or ask to see you, no matter how interested they are, the chances are 1 in 100 that they'll make the request. So here are some of the better closing techniques I know and use aside from those others I've already illustrated in the preceding examples.

Closing on the appointment

If the goal for your telephone conversation was to secure an appointment with your prospect, then you need to judge the most appropriate time to ask for that appointment. If you cannot sell something over the telephone, then remember that all you are selling is an appointment. So as soon as possible during the conversation, when the prospect has warmed to you, is showing an interest and is asking more questions, that is the time to ask for the appointment. The more you say and the more questions you answer, the more you risk giving the prospect a reason for not seeing you. Here are various ways you can ask for the appointment:

The alternative date close

It is always better to ask a question that doesn't give your prospect the option to give a 'yes' or 'no' answer. Instead use the alternative date close. For example:

"Jane, you obviously have some interest in what we may be able to do for you. Aside from the fact that there are many more questions I would need to ask you, and questions I'm sure you would like to ask me, I really do like to meet with potential clients and get a better feel for their business. I'm free next Tuesday at 4pm or Friday at 11am. Which of those dates would be better for you to meet with me?" (Silent close).

Or

"Robert, I appreciate there's lots more you need to know and the best way for you to get a complete picture of what we might be able to do for you is for us to meet and let me show you some examples of what we have been able to achieve for

other companies like yours. I'm free for 45 minutes next Tuesday at 4pm or Friday at 11am. Which of those dates would be better for you?" (Silent close).

Or

"Robert, the very best way for you to appreciate what this can do to increase your production/increase sales/ reduce overheads is to see this working. I could bring round a demo model for you to test next Tuesday at 4pm or Friday at 11am. Which of those would be better for you?" (Silent close).

You can also use the 'alternative venue' close – in other words, 'your place or mine?' For example:

"Robert, the very best way for you to appreciate what this can do to increase your production/increase sales/ reduce overheads is to see this working. I could bring round a demo model for you to test or you could visit our offices and get a much better feel for the system and how we operate. Which would you prefer?" (Silent Close).

Or

"Robert, I appreciate there's lots more you need to know and the best way for you to get a complete picture of what we might be able to do for you is for us to meet and let me show you some examples of what we have been able to achieve for other companies like yours. I'm happy to come and see you at your office or would you prefer to come to us and get a complete picture of our set up, how we operate and meet

some of the other key personnel who would be working with me on your account?" (Silent Close).

Get the prospect to ask for the appointment

This close is the least stressful to both the salesperson and the prospect. Here is what you say after you have generated sufficient interest:

"John, you obviously believe there could be several advantages to taking a closer look at this and it's not really possible to cover a great deal more over the telephone. So what would you like me to do now?" (Silent Close) OR *"So what happens next?"* (Silent Close).

You have taken all the pressure off yourself but you have not put any pressure on the prospect either. You have not asked them for the appointment and have given them a choice. Of course the only sensible choice they can make is the one you want.

Tailor the 'alternative date' and 'alternative venue' closes to your specific product or service. Write some examples on the following pages or separate sheets and practice and rehearse them.

ALTERNATIVE DATE & VENUE CLOSES

Cold Calling

Closing the sale

Getting the prospect to place an order is obviously more difficult than closing on an appointment; you are asking for a firm commitment and, in many cases, money up-front. So before you attempt to close the sale, in most cases you need to be almost certain your prospect is ready to buy before you close.

Here are a variety of closes you can use:

Get the prospect to close the sale

As with closing on the appointment, this close is the least stressful to both the salesperson and the prospect. Here is what you say when you believe they could be ready to buy:

"John, On the basis of what we've discussed so far, are you 100% certain that this would work for you?"

(Yes - I think so)

"So what would you like me to do now?" (Silent Close) OR *"So what happens next?"* (Silent Close).

Ask for the money

Getting an agreement on the pricing is another method for closing a sale. Now I know that many salespeople do not like asking for money, or even talking about money, and when the time comes the salesperson begins to get a little panicky and the easy flow of the conversation starts to stall.

Providing you have exposed sufficient pain and the prospect seems eager to deal with it, why should you have a problem asking for the money? Your prospect certainly was not expecting the solution to come without a cost and opening up the discussion on it as early as possible can also enable a prompt close. Therefore you can simply say, "The investment required to solve these problems is going to be in the region of (£XXX). Is that going to be OK with you?" (Silent Close).

If they respond with a "Yes", then you ask for the money which could be asking for a credit card payment or where and who to send an invoice to or the process for setting up an account, or it could be the process they go through to place an order with you.

Turning a question into a sale

This is another very powerful closing technique and there are frequent opportunities to use it during many sales presentations. How can you turn a question from a prospect into a close? Let us look at a few examples:

Prospect: *Does it come in red?*

You: *Would you like it in red?*

Prospect: *Yes.* [They have bought]

You: *How would you like to pay for this?*

Prospect: Is *there a discount if I buy a larger quantity?*

Salesperson: *Would you like a larger quantity if I can get you a discount?*

Prospect: *Yes.* [They have bought – subject to the discount being acceptable]

Prospect: *Can I pay for the 12 month series of ads monthly?*

Salesperson: *Would you like to pay for them monthly?*

Prospect: *Yes.* [They have bought]

The deadline close

There will often be times when you have a limited number of end-of-range products, or when you are offering a discount on a service because your company is going through a particularly quiet patch.

Here are some examples of deadline closes that have been presented to me:

"Mr King, the CRM programme which we've been discussing and which you've agreed would work for you is going up in price by 19% in a few days time – I don't have the specific date. So if you are looking to save a considerable sum of money, I'd suggest you place an order now. How would you be planning to pay for this?"

AND

"Mr King, I have inside information from the sales department at the manufacturers that this model is soon to be replaced by the updated version, which is going to cost some £250 more. I'm prepared to offer you one of the last few of this model, and with an additional five percent discount. You'd need to place an order right away to take advantage of this. Would you want us to invoice this or would you prefer to settle by credit card?"

The secondary question close

Use this close when you are fairly certain that your prospect is willing to accept your proposition and all that is necessary is to put it to bed quickly. The technique is based on posing the major buying question first, then immediately by-passing it with another question of lesser importance which is much easier to make a decision on than the main purchase. Here are a few examples:

Salesman: *I think we have covered everything now Mr Prospect. We just need to take your credit card details. By the way, will you be designing your own ad or would you like us to do it for you?*

Prospect: Our graphics department will put it together [They've bought it]

Salesman: *Thank you.*

Salesperson: *From what we have discussed so far Mr Prospect, I think the computer with 1000 gigabytes is going to be most suitable for you. Would you prefer it in black or silver?*

Prospect: *I would prefer black.* [They've bought it]

Salesperson: *From what we've discussed, the Bahamas seems to be the ideal holiday for you and your family. Will you be paying by cheque or credit card?*

Prospect: *By credit card.* [They've bought it]

The psychology behind this type of close is very simple. Giving the prospect the opportunity to agree to some very minor point means that the major decision, and the most expensive one, is taken out of the picture completely. Buyer resistance vanishes with this style of close.

Tailor these closes to your specific product or service. Write them below or on a separate sheet now and practice and rehearse them.

CLOSE THE SALE QUESTIONS

Summary

You have everything in this program to become World-Class at cold calling for setting appointments and closing sales on the telephone. Practice and rehearse these techniques and you will never look back.

For more intensive training developed for your specific product or service, contact Bruce King through his website at www.bruceking.co.uk

Cold Calling

More books by Bruce King

Full details on his website at

www.bruceking.co.uk

Psycho-Selling
Double Your Income From Sales In 8 Weeks
(Crown House Publishing)

How To Double Your Sales
The ultimate master class in how to
sell anything to anyone
(Financial Times Series)

Winning Sales Referrals
A step-by-step process for winning all the sales you
could ever want, just from referrals
(SoderPalm Publishing)

Smash Your Goals
How to win the battle in your mind between Einstein and
Frankenstein and achieve great success and happiness
(Crown House Publishing)

www.ingramcontent.com/pod-product-compliance
Lightning Source LLC
Chambersburg PA
CBHW070812180526
45168CB00002B/587